The World Secret of Fatima
Flying Saucers and Beyond

Michael X
Alfred Steber

Saucerian Publisher
Original Sources in Ufology

ISBN:978-1-955087-43-8

9 781955 087438

© 2023,Saucerian Publisher

Micheal X aka Michael Barton with his wife.

Prologue

Saucerian Publisher was founded with the mission of promoting books in Science Fiction. Our vision is to preserve the legacy of literary history by reprint editions of books which have already been exhausted or are difficult to obtain. Our goal is to help readers, educators and researchers by bringing back original publications that are difficult to find at reasonable price, while preserving the legacy of universal knowledge. This book is an authentic reproduction of the original printed text in shades of gray and may contain minor errors due to the aging of the pages.This title was originally published in 1960.

Michael Barton, aka Michael X. Barton adopted the pen name Michael X. to conceal his identity. In the mid-1950s, Michael Barton took a pilgrimage to Giant Rock. Inspired by George Van Tassel's apparent ability to channel ETs, Barton embraced the notion that the universe is composed of "mind stuff" that can transmit thought vibrations. On the historic night of May 22nd, 1955—his gaze fixed determinedly on Venus—Barton projected a "vibratory beam of light" and, using what he called "space telepathy". Based on his "closed contact" with aliens, he wrote: *Secrets of Higher Contact* in (1959).

In *The World Secret of Fatima,* published in 1962, Michael X explored the Fatima message.In the prologue of this book he pointed out that: *The Fatima message unveils the great Secret of Beingness. That is why it can help you, me, and every one of earth's 3 billion souls... now. For it teaches all of us that there exists in this universe One Law which no man can ever outwit, for it is the Law of Being. It has three parts. (1) Be a Life Spirit, (2) Do Love all of Life, and (3) Havē wisdom, knowingness and the Truth. .*

Editor
Saucerian Publisher, 2023

THE WORLD SECRET OF FATIMA

By

MICHAEL X

This is an Educational and Inspirational Treatise. It is especially intended for study by NEW-AGE minded persons everywhere. The following Seven Chapters are contained herein:

INTRODUCTION

TODAY -- at this very hour in which you and I live -- man is attempting to use Life-Energy for a unique, scientific purpose. He wants to explore outer space... see what the Moon is like...find out if the planets are inhabited and if so, by what manner of creatures?

If he finds other human beings living upon distant planets in space, dauntless earthman will try to communicate with them. But what he does after the first "communication lines" have been opened to other planets is a subject which provides genuine "food for thought".

Why? Because earthman has not yet learned how to get along peaceably with other earthmen on his own home planet earth. From the dawn of earth's history it has been a constant case of "nation against nation, brother against brother". And this same inability to "get along" -- to understand -- to help our brothers and sisters in spite of differences in creed, race, color or beliefs, is still one of earthman's biggest failings and regrets.

"THE WORLD SECRET OF FATIMA" is something we ought to know; not only for our own individual good -- vital though that is -- but also for the good of all human and yes, sub-human, beings wherever we may find them to be. Whether we discover them living upon some far-off planet or in some near or distant nation on the earth is of no consequence. Can we grant them "beingness"? That is it.

The Fatima Message unveils the great Secret of Beingness. That is why it can help you, me, and every one of earth's 3 billion souls...now. For it teaches all of us that there exists in this universe One Law which no man can ever outwit, for it is the Law of Being. It has three parts. (1) Be a Life Spirit, (2) Do Love all of Life, and (3) Have wisdom, knowingness and the Truth.

This One Law is a Divine Axiom, infinitely real. It is fulfilled only by demonstrating the second postulant: Do Love all of Life. Affinity for all Life is what the Divine Mother herself personifies. Earthman must realize that affinity. For the Divine Madonna tells us plainly -- but with deepest concern and compassion -- that if we BE alive, but do not LOVE, we shall not HAVE the Higher Consciousness...Wisdom...Truth.

With brotherly Love and true appreciation for the Real and Wonderful You, I place this book gently in your hands. May You unfold its Secret!

MICHAEL X

THE MYSTERIOUS LADY APPEARS

Chapter One

Editor's note to Reader: The following treatise which you are about to study, is the actual transcription from a tape-recording of a lecture given by Michael X to live audiences in the State of California. To set the desired high mood, and lift the group vibration, Michael X began by asking all to join him in the following prayer:

"HEAVENLY Father-Mother God, we ask Thy blessing of Life, Love and Light upon every soul in this room tonight. Let Thy Life, Love and Light fill the minds, the hearts, the souls and the bodies of each and every one of us here tonight. Lift us in vibration so that we may comprehend the wonderful truth that only Thou can give to us. We ask that our vibrations be lifted into a higher frequency this evening, that we may penetrate into the deeper mysteries which must be known before our earthly schooling be complete.

"We ask that every soul here, move forward into the NEW-AGE boldly...and by Thy grace break the Rule of Ahriman and the forces of darkness on this planet. May Thy Plan be manifested in us. Amen!"

TONIGHT I'd like you to follow me in your mind, while I weave a mental picture before your mind's eye, so that you may see some of humanity's past history and intermediary stages up to the present time. Are you ready to begin? Good! While you watch certain hidden processes unfold, perhaps you will more clearly understand why things are as they are in the world today, and the underlying causes for much of the "confusion" and "mystery" that we see about us everywhere. Follow me closely if you will, please.

What we are going to talk about tonight deals with a WORLD SECRET. That Secret involves -- among other things -- the mystery of the unidentified flying objects; a subject that is even less understood today than when the phenomenon first began many years ago.

Some of these mysterious objects in our skies -- the UFO's -- a very great many of them, in fact, are not built upon this earth. We might look upon them -- if we will -- as spaceships which are acting as intermediaries between worlds. And if we can carry our thinking one short step further we find ourselves with the consideration that they are intermediaries from more advanced worlds. That is, they are intermediaries from higher density worlds to a lower density world, and that they carry spiritual messengers who are bringing a particular spiritual message to this world. And we

find that when we look backwards in time, that whenever the world was in a very dire predicament, that is when there were appearances of the UFO's and the beings that come in these grand craft.

In my opinion the WORLD SECRET OF FATIMA can only be fully understood in relation to the mystery of the Unidentified Flying Objects. One looks at both sides of the coin, as it were. That is the proper, scientific way to look at Reality. This topic we are searching into tonight is big, vital and very important. That is why we are going to use both intellect and intuition as guides. and with these helpmates, turn "mystery" into "knowingness"!

The first big question we should face is -- why? Why has the essential truth on such tremendously important topics as those we are now viewing with wide-open eyes, been kept a deep, dark SECRET?

Because, my friend, there is a world conspiracy to keep the truth from people on this planet, and tonight we'll discover why that is so, what is really back of it all...and how we can "break the Rule" of those Forces that would keep us down and submerged in a material darkness that suffocates the very Spirit in us!

The FATIMA STORY is intimately related to present time happenings in our world, but in order to get a positive perspective on it we'll have to leave present time briefly, and travel back a few years to October 13, 1917.

Now picture with me and follow with me if you will please, a tremendous crowd of people -- people just like you and me -- all moving slowly into a large valley, a sheltered valley in a little town near Fatima, Portugal, in that year 1917. Thousands of good men and women of all ages, from all walks of life, are wending their way with us (let's imagine we are there with them) into a great open area of the countryside called the Cova da Iria.

And why? Why are they gathering here? Because they have all been promised something...something quite out of the ordinary. They have been promised that a "miracle" would be shown to them at this particular place. Today they would see a miracle here.

Look around you now and you'll see quite a crowd. Seventy-thousand or more persons are assembling around us in the Cova. All are in a state of high expectation. The report has gone all around the whole countryside that at high noon today, October 13th, 1917, there will be -- positively -- a miracle of such power and impact that it will cause untold thousands of human beings to believe in the living reality of a being called Mary, and to believe that there is something more to life than simply a material, effect side that we see with our physical eyes.

There is a spiritual basis to life. In fact, the very foundation of the world is spiritual, and these people, many of whom

are simple peasants, know that instinctively. That is why they've
come here. They've come from every village, town and city nearby
for miles around. By now the Cova da Iria is thickly jammed with
every type of humanity...in spite of the fact that all day there
have been threatening signs of rain in the sky. And when it rains
in this part of the country, it's usually a real downpour.

Oh, Oh, there's the rain now! It comes pouring down, drenching all of us thoroughly...soaking our clothing all the way through
to the skin. Rain can be a terrible nuisance sometimes. Amidst
the battering rainfall we grab a quick look at people around us.
To put it mildly, they seem upset by this bad weather. What do you
suppose is running through their minds this instant?

May be they are wondering if all this business of a predicted
"miracle" is really just a great big illusion. Mass hypnosis. An
impossibility in a world as modern as ours. May be the three little children -- Lucy, Jacinta and Francisco -- who had been the
ones responsible for the "rumor" that a miracle would be forthcom-
ing today, had simply been having a pipe-dream. May be nothing
"miraculous" was going to happen at all.

May be. But it is early yet...far too early to backtrack for
home. We must see if anything unusual will occur. An event such
as this that had been promised is worth waiting for, because if it
does take place on schedule...our very lives may be transformed.
Who cares about the drenching, downpouring rain? Not us.

Now, suddenly, we'll leave that picture, and flash back to it
later. But keep the feeling of it, if you will, as we now move into the part of our story which reveals the background for the big
scene we've just experienced. Now we are going to cast our mental
spotlight upon the three little children who caused all of this
furore, and who got these 70,000 adult people out into the Cova in
the pouring rainstorm. What was it about these children -- Lucy
Santos and her cousins Jacinta and Francisco -- what did they SEE
prior to this gathering, that caused all of these people to gather
together out there? You and I realize that a hugh crowd like this
is not going to be motivated like this unless there is a reason.

Something that these little children had done or said, had
touched this great crowd of people...convinced them of...Well, I
shall tell you the story because it is one of the most interesting
and significant stories that has ever been told in our times.

First of all, I'd like to say that "Fatima" means "Lady" in
Arabic. And in the French Etymological Dictionary it states that
Fatima is "she who brings peace". In times of turmoil, violence
and the threat of sudden, total annihilation of great nations and
millions of men, women and children..peace is what the world must
understand and achieve or civilization as we see it will perish.

Now let's leave 1917 and move backwards on the time-track one
year, to 1916 when the episode of the three children really begins.
In that year 1916, Lucy Santos and her two little cousins, Jacinta
and Francisco Marto were out one day in the field tending sheep,
near the small town where they lived. Aljustrel was the name of
this town, and it was fairly close to Fatima, in Portugal.

While they were in the fields tending their sheep, the sky
clouded over and soon it started to rain. The children were near
a rocky cliff at the time, and since the cliff happened to have a
rather spacious cave near the top, they decided to climb the cliff,
go into the cave and get out of the rain. So they began to climb.
But, just as they began to climb they noticed that the rain had
suddenly stopped falling. The wind had also stopped blowing, and
there was a dazzling light on the horizon, like a lightning flash.

Watching the skies, Lucy and her two companions were simply
astounded to see an extremely bright light, apparently globular in
shape, coming towards the spot where they stood. It made absolutely no sound as it approached them. Upon reaching the place where
the children were, the silent globe of light stopped motionless.
Out of the brilliant globe, extended a kind of beam of light in
which the form of a young man, gently descended to the earth. If
you will imagine a very youthful being whose very body, handsome
beyond earthly conception, appears to be emanating light...and
whose eyes sparkle with an extraordinary super-intelligence...you
will have some idea of what this unusual being looked like.

"Fear not," this celestial being said to Lucy and the others,
"I am the Angel of Peace. Pray with me, children, like this. O my
God, I believe, I adore, I hope, and I love you. I ask pardon for
all those who do not believe, who do not adore, who do not hope,
and who do not love you!" Three times he repeated this prayer.

"Pray like this, for the hearts of the higher beings, Christ
and Mary, will be touched by your prayers and will respond by
bringing something wonderful into your lives."

With that, the celestial being ascended the light beam into
the globe, gravitated upward and was soon out of sight. In recount-
ing the experience later, Lucy revealed that she and Jacinta and
Francisco were so overwhelmed by the event that they threw themselves upon the ground and repeated the Angel's Prayer for hours
after he had gone. At last they got up and made their way home.

One important detail must now be mentioned. Although Francisco
saw the celestial being, as did Jacinta and Lucy, he was not able
to hear what was spoken by the angel. However, by listening to
the words of the prayer which the girls kept repeating, Francisco
was soon able to learn it and repeat it also. The same year, the
angel visited the children twice more, inspiring them greatly.
After these amazing experiences all was quiet in the lives of
Lucy, Jacinta and Francisco until May 13 of the year 1917. It

was at the Cova da Iria while the children were out tending their sheep again, that it happened. Suddenly on the horizon there was the familiar flash of light. This time, however, as the bright globe of light came down out of the clouds near then, a beautiful lady descended via the light beam, to where they stood.

"Do not be afraid," the lady said to them, "I shall not harm you. I come from Heaven. I come to ask you to meet me here at the Cova six times in succession on the 13th of each month, at the same hour, and in October I shall tell you who I am and what I expect of you. After the six appearances, I shall return here again a seventh time."

Then the mysterious lady re-entered her globe of light, gravitated upwards swiftly and silently and quickly vanished from sight.

During this strange appearance of the lady, Lucy Santos alone was able to both see and hear the lady. It was Lucy who conversed with her. Jacinta heard the lady speaking to Lucy, and Francisco only heard Lucy answering the lady. You see, many young children quite frequently have their inner spiritual eyes and ears open up until a certain age. When that age is reached and the individual goes into denser, material living, then the "spiritual sight and hearing" is dulled and no more is the spiritual world looked into. Lucy had her inner eye and ear wide open, and she saw and heard everything the lady said to her.

Quite naturally and humanly, the children, when they got home, began telling their parents about the strange experiences. Their parents, for considerations of their own, were not enthusiastic. They were more than a little upset by the news. "Don't tell anybody that," they warned the children, "or they will think you are crazy!" But it is difficult to keep these things hushed up.

Secrets do have a way of getting around. And the good folks, those whose soul-life is not asleep, they hear these secrets and these remarkable stories..and..by God's grace they wonder.

For this reason, when next month, June 13th, rolled around, and, as scheduled, the children went to meet the beautiful lady at the Cova, there were about forty or fifty of the villagers waiting there. They were curious to see if there was anything to this.

At the expected time the lady appeared and said to the three little ones: "Jesus will use you to make me better known and more loved. He wishes to establish throughout the world the devotion to my Immaculate Heart." That was the message she gave to the children at that time. So they went home, revealed to a few persons what had happened on June 13th, and said that they had seen the lady again and that she said she wished to establish devotion to her Immaculate Heart. The townspeople listened and...I am sorry to say...laughed.

For the most part, they, the townspeople of Aljustrel and of Fatima, were not much "impressed" by the childrens' reports of a mysterious globe of light and a beautiful lady. Many of the people considered the tales to be outright lying on the part of the children. Others feared that the devil was back of it all. Some of the leaders in the community hurriedly consulted among themselves and then cautioned the children to be careful.

"Better watch out!" they warned, "This thing you say has happened may all be a trick of the devil. It is most likely evil and dangerous, and so we do not think it wise for you to go around telling these stories and holding meetings at the Cova!"

Yet, in all of us there is something that wishes to believe. The townsfolk had that "something" in them, also..and, moreover, they had another ingredient in their makeup that urged them compulsively to pay a visit to the Cova. Curiosity -- that was it! So the many curious ones made a bee line to the Cova da Iria to see for themselves just what might happen on July 13th. This time the public turnout was something terrific. This time 5,000 persons turned out, in contrast to the mere 50 at the June meeting.

Picture it. Five thousand hopeful individuals waiting at the Cova. Waiting for Lucy Santos and her two little cousins, and for the appearance of the lady. Each one hoping against hope that it was not a joke, but real, and that they would be permitted to see the lady for themselves.

The most ancient civilizations and religions known to earth's humanity, tell us that there exists a mysterious lady who has appeared in a seemingly miraculous manner to man ever since man was on this planet. Long before the advent of the various masculine figures of the great World Teachers -- Hermes, Buddha, Jesus, etc. -- our world has known of this magnificent, perfected feminine being. Many are the teachings about "the Ancient Mother", "the Celestial Virgin", "the Mother of Two Truths", "the Divine Madonna".

All religions carry the idea of a "World Mother". Zoroaster or Zarathustra told about the "Celestial Virgin" to the Persians. It is the most ancient in origin. Let me explain briefly this great tradition, for it is, to most earthlings, unknown.

Back of all worlds, all systems, is the mother of all life. She is called the Ancient Divine Mother because she, as principle, has "beingness" which pervades the universe. In the primal morning of earth, she declared that Mother-Love, the feminine principle was co-equal with Father-Wisdom, the masculine principle. When man unfolds a higher perception of Deity, he perceives this dual nature of all life. From the Ancient Mother sprang forth a Divine Mother for every constellation. Each solar system is under the mandate of a Divine Mother, who at the necessary times, sends her hand-maiden from her heavens of light to the earth planet.

8

THIS IS THE FATIMA MESSAGE

Chapter Two

When Lucy, Jacinta and Francisco arrived at the Cova on July 13, 1917, they were amazed to see some 5,000 people waiting there to greet them and to wait for the Lady to appear. They did not have to wait long. Soon there came a bright flash of light on the horizon. Then the anxious crowd saw what seemed to be a brilliant white cloud floating downward.

The "cloud" stopped motionless close to a tree near which the three children were standing. Then it was noticed by the onlookers that Lucy Santos was "in contact" with some individual whom they could not see. Furthermore, Lucy was now conversing in all earnestness with that mysterious personage.

As the child continued to communicate with the being, a fervor of almost ecstatic excitement swept through the multitude. With this feeling came a sense of positive realism... the Lady had appeared to the children. Although "she" was of a vibration much too high to be seen by the crowd, they intuitively sensed now that the Celestial Lady was, in all reality, there.

Lucy took the opportunity then to register a small complaint. Could the Lady do anything to somehow persuade Lucy's own mother and her church pastor as well, that all of these beautiful apparitions were really true and not simply figments of imagination?

"Continue these monthly meetings on the 13th of each month," responded the Lady, "and in October I shall work a true miracle."

She then revealed things in which you and I and the world of today are most interested in, for the simple reason that we are -- all of us -- involved in the vital world event proclaimed by the FATIMA MESSAGE. We may admit it or we may not. But the fact remains that the SECRET of Fatima -- both the publicly revealed and the unrevealed portions of it -- touch us vitally where we "live".

This is so because the Fatima Message deals with exceedingly realistic subjects such as: War -- Peace -- Russia -- Communism -- Faith -- persecutions and martyrdoms -- changes coming upon Earth. These matters touch all human lives in one degree or another. As you study THE FATIMA MESSAGE, I would have you bear in mind this thought. The Message itself contains universal truth -- principle -- which goes far beyond the boundaries and scope of an earthly church or established religion. Its truth is for everyone.

The basic, essential "FATIMA MESSAGE" of Our Lady is this:

"If people do what I shall tell you, many souls shall be saved, and there will be peace in the world. World War I is going to end. But if they do not stop offending God, another and worse war will begin in the reign of Pius XI. When you shall see a night illumined by an unknown light, know that it is a sign that God gives you, that He is going to punish the world for its crimes. The punishment shall come in the form of war, hunger, persecution of the church and of the Holy Father.

(On January 25, 1938 a strange light, an "unknown light", was seen by Lucy in the northern sky. Europe and a portion of our North America were treated to a fabulous display of Northern Lights unlike any Aurora Borealis ever before seen.)

"To prevent this chastisement, I shall come to ask the consecration of Russia to my Immaculate Heart, and the communion of the faithful on the first Saturdays, as reparation. If this is done, Russia will be converted and there will be peace. If not, Russia will spread her errors throughout the world...provoking wars and persecutions of the church. The good will be martyred and various nations will be annihilated."

This word, "annihilated", is the strongest word that could possibly be used. Note that Our Lady used it back in 1917, long before Communism as an ideology was considered a threat of any great seriousness to the world. Long before "World Communism" got its stranglehold on humanity, the Lady predicted: "Various nations will be annihilated", and what is the fact today? Look, if you will, at the basic timetable formulated by Lenin for World Conquest. Add it up. Its record is inescapable fact; its speed frightening!

In 1917, by skillful use of propaganda and mass terror, the Communists seized control of Soviet Russia. Lenin set the Communist timetable with these prophetic words: "First we shall take Eastern Europe. Next the masses of Asia!" By 1949, Stalin had fulfilled Lenin's prophecy. All of Eastern Europe had fallen under Communist control. Then Stalin indoctrinated the masses of China with the ideology of Communism. In 1951, Tibet came under Red control. In 1954 North Vietnam was taken over by the Communists. In 1961 they grabbed Cuba via Castro, and are now holding it..in our hemisphere!

Lenin -- in his predictions -- has also said: "We shall encircle...the United States...it will fall like an overripe fruit into our hands!" The Communists have plans to take over other countries according to their timetable, which projects further into the near future. So far, their timetable is running on schedule.

According to a recent report by American Opinion magazine, at least 43% of the world's total population is already under Communist control. 28% is fifty per cent under Communist rule, making a

grand percentage of 71% of mankind that is now under that system. The remainder -- 29% --is teetering on the brink of Communism, not fully realizing what Communism means, or what is NOW HAPPENING.

THE FATIMA MESSAGE continues: "In the end, my Immaculate Heart will triumph. The Holy Father will consecrate Russia to me; she will be converted, and a certain period of peace will be granted to the world. In Portugal, the dogma of the faith will be kept always. Tell this to none except to Francisco."

Then Our Lady told the third -- and highly controversial -- part of the secret to Lucy. It was written down by Lucy, placed in a sealed envelope, and given to the Bishop of Leiria. He put it in the archives of the church, to be opened in 1960.

Now let's move on to the next month -- August, 1917 -- in this great episode of three little children, the mysterious appearances of the beautiful Lady, and the strange Secret of Fatima.

August 13th was the scheduled time of the next meeting. This time the crowd was more than three times as big as before. Nearly 18,000 persons had gathered at the Cova for the event. However, all was NOT due to go smoothly. The magistrate of Fatima had other ideas. He happened to be an atheist and he had managed to acquire a great deal of power in that little town. For reasons of his own, he didn't approve of mass-meetings of people at the Cova da Iria, meetings which were caused of course by the wide circulation of the children's report of "apparitions of the Lady".

The magistrate determined to put an end to the whole business. Jumping into his carriage, he drove out to the Cova and soon located the three little children, Lucy, Jacinto and Francisco. By some cunning pretext, the magistrate got the children into his carriage and then drove off with them at top speed toward town.

There were, however, many onlookers among the crowd at the Cova who had been watching this little scene. When they realized what was happening, some of them stoned the carriage. But to no avail. It was too late to stop him from stealing the children.

The wily magistrate succeeded in driving away with the three children in the carriage, and as soon as he reached town, went straight to the prison. He put the three children in the prison -- behind locked doors and barred windows -- so that they would be unable to keep their regular appointment with the mysterious Lady at the Cova da Iria. His plan was to talk to each child privately -- separated from the others -- and persuade them to change their story, even if he had to threaten their lives.

So the magistrate took Lucy first, to another cell apart from Jacinto and Francisco, and very gently said: "If you do not confess to everyone that your story is false, I will boil you in oil!"

Lucy -- much to the magistrate's confusion -- looked him straight in the eye. The Lady, she said, had told her there would be days like this... that there would be some very unpleasant experiences to live through -- but that if they were true to her, and did not deny her, some marvelous things would happen. Lucy then announced firmly that she would not, for any reason, deny the Lady nor the true fact of her appearances at the Cova.

Hearing this, the magistrate was furious. However, he did not boil Lucy in oil as he had threatened to do. He thought perhaps he might have better luck with the other two children. So he went to each individually, after separating them from one another, and he threatened each one with terrible punishment if they refused to deny their story of the mysterious and beautiful Lady.

His luck was a big zero. The apparitions which Jacinta and Francisco had witnessed along with Lucy, were simply too real, too beautiful and too important in their young lives. Alongside those experiences, those "contacts with higher reality", an experience such as being "boiled in oil" was of no real consequence.

Failing to change their minds, the magistrate finally brought all three children back to the same room where they were again reunited. Each child had thought that his companions had been boiled in oil and killed, and so upon seeing them alive, was overjoyed.

Making sure that the appointed time, August 13th, was well past, so that the children would miss their scheduled appointment with the Lady at the Cova, the magistrate then released them. It was impossible for the magistrate to keep the news from spreading. It spread like wildfire -- first through the entire crowd assembled and waiting at the Cova. That crowd totaled 18,000 persons. You can imagine just how greatly disappointed and angry they must have been by the actions of the magistrate.

Then -- with gathering momentum -- the word spread to every neighboring town and village for hundreds of miles around. You can't really beat word-of-mouth advertising, you know. And who can stop good people from talking? They felt cheated. What the magistrate had done was clearly and simply an injustice. Although the crowd at the Cova in August at length dispersed as night grew near and still no sign of Lucy, Jacinta and Francisco, there was no power on earth that could have kept them from talking about it.

The magistrate had won the first round. He had imprisoned the children. He had prevented them from going to the Cova. But doubtless you have noticed in your own life experience, that actions like that of the magistrate of Fatima have a way of "backfiring". Evil may sometimes stimulate good. In this instance, the negative purpose of the magistrate was being defeated by the very action he himself had taken. For the news had got around. Many more persons were thereby alerted to the next big meeting in September.

12

MIRACLE IN THE SKY

Chapter Three

When September 13th arrived, 30,000 persons turned out at the Cova da Iria, for the next appearance of the Lady. Every person there knew all about the magistrate's action of imprisoning the three children, and just to show their ob jection to his "interference" they were assembled now -- en masse -- 30,000 eager souls, at the scheduled meeting place.

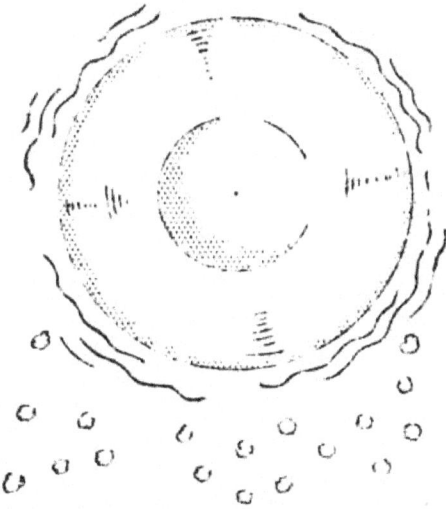

This time, the children, Lucy and her two little cousins, were safely protected by the crowd. There was not the slightest possible chance for the highly unpopular magistrate of Fatima to prevent the three little ones from keeping their appointment with the Celestial Lady.

As the massive crowd waited, certain signs of the Lady's presence began to be noticed by Lucy. The atmosphere held an unusual warmth and the clouds above the multitude were forming at a much lower altitude than normally. In a few minutes there appeared, not a small cloud, but this time a great globe of light. The globe began to descend to earth near the three children. As it did so, a shower of small white petals fell from the brilliant sphere. Oddly enough, the "petals" disappeared before reaching the ground. (UFO students will recognize this phenomenon. It is known as "angel hair".)

The Lady, dressed in her shimmering white mantle, stepped out from the globe of Light and was perfectly visible to Lucy, Jacinta and Francisco. She reassured the children, telling them that on October 13th, date of her next appearance, she would perform a miracle, as she had promised, and that others from Heaven would appear.

Two members of the crowd had given Lucy two letters and a bottle of eau de cologne prior to the meeting and had asked her to present those articles to the Celestial Lady. So at an opportune moment, Lucy attempted to hand them to the Lady, who responded by saying that she appreciated the fine gesture but that "none of that is necessary in heaven."

During this apparition -- as previously -- a wave of joyous elation and sense of reality swept through the great crowd of human beings at the Cova. All shared in the thrill of the event.

Then Our Lady brought the apparition to a conclusion, calmly reentered the great globe of light and instantly it began to rise smoothly, silently high into the eastern sky and vanished. Lucy motioned to the crowd and the 30,000 wended their way homeward.

October 13th -- day of the next meeting -- came at last. On this very special day of days, a "miracle" would be performed for the special benefit of scoffers, skeptics and general "unbelievers". What kind of miracle? Nobody knew, nor for that matter, cared. Something miraculous, out of the ordinary, had been promised and that was sufficient to cause quite a stir.

Now let us return to that October scene which I first set in Chapter One. At the Cova da Iria, an immense crowd had assembled. Most of the people who had been to the previous month's meeting had persuaded one or more new persons to come with them now. So there were over 70,000 individuals assembled. You will recall it had begun to rain and these 70,000 people are waiting in the drenching rainstorm for some unusual phenomenon to occur.

There was a priest who, like many others, had slept overnight at the Cova in order to be ready for the events on the big day. He was keeping an eye upon the three children so that, in case there was some hitch and no miracle happened, he could protect them and get them safely away from the crowd. For it is difficult to predict what a crowd will do when it is disappointed on a great matter.

This priest was tagging along with Lucy and the other two, frequently looking at his watch. "What time is Mary supposed to appear?" he inquired of the children.

"Twelve o'clock," answered Lucy.

"Good!" said the priest, and looked again at his watch. One minute of twelve. He waited tensely -- rain pouring down upon his face -- for high noon. Twelve o'clock. Still no sign. Another anxious minute passed...two minutes...three. Suddenly he cried: "Let's get out of here! Nothing is going to happen, it was all a dream." He reached for Lucy's hand.

"No!" Lucy shouted. "Our Lady told me she would come, and she will." Lucy refused to budge a foot. Impressed by her sense of certainty, the priest said: "Well, all right. I shall wait."

Just then there was a sudden flash on the horizon. The rain stopped. A strange, almost oven-like warmth was beginning to pervade the air. It had a peculiar drying effect that was startling. Soaking wet clothes of the multitude became comfortably dry in a matter of minutes. Lucy pointed out these unusual signs to the priest and announced that the Lady was near and about to make her scheduled appearance. The long-awaited time had arrived.

I shall now let some of the actual eye-witnesses describe to you what really happened on that historic day; for they were present at the scene and gave written accounts of what they saw. We shall hear the account of Maria da Capelina, first: "The sun cast different colors, yellow, blue and white. It trembled constantly.

It looked like a revolving ball of fire falling upon the people."

One of the newspapers in Lisbon had sent a reporter to cover the big event at the Cova. The paper was the "O Seculo" and the reporter was Avelino d'Almeida. On October 17th, the following article describing the "miracle" was published:

"A spectacle unique and incredible if one had not been a witness of it personally. One can see the immense crowd turn toward the 'sun' which reveals itself free of the clouds in full view."

(NOTE: We must bear in mind, my friend, that this spectacle of what seemed to be the sun, was misinterpreted by the people. They naturally assumed that the object they saw was the sun of our solar system, moving out of its orbit and gyrating around in the sky above their heads. Therefore they called it "the miracle of the sun". In reality it was not the sun. What was it?)

"The great star of day makes one think of a silver plaque, and it is possible to look straight at it without the least discomfort. It does not burn, nor does it blind. Rather it might be like an eclipse. But now bursts forth a colossal clamor and we hear the nearest spectators crying 'Miracle! Miracle! Marvel! Marvel!' Before the astonished eyes of the people whose attitude now carries us back to biblical times, and who full of terror, heads uncovered, gaze into the blue of the sky, the 'sun' has trembled, and the 'sun' has made some brusque movements, unprecedented and outside of all cosmic law. 'The sun has danced' according to the expression of the peasants.

"An old man turns toward the sun and recites the credo from beginning to end. I see him afterward addressing those about him who have kept their hats on, begging them vehemently to uncover before so extraordinary a demonstration of the existence of God. Similar scenes are repeated in all places at the Cova."

Another first-hand witness was Dr. Carlos Mendez, president of the city of Tores Noves. His report was as follows:

"The rain stopped." (NOTE: This is unusual. Even more amazing is the fact that a drying-warmth pervaded the atmosphere at the near approach of the strange flying object in the sky.)

"The clouds split up into tatters, thin transparent strips. The 'sun' was visible as a crown of fire, empty in the middle. It went around itself (NOTE: This is clearly the action of a UFO or celestial spaceship, not the physical sun) and moved across the sky. It would be seen behind the clouds and in between them, rolling around horizontally. Some cried, 'I believe!'; others cried 'Forgive!'. The crowd prayed in terror as they watched." (NOTE: The children and some others also saw the Holy Family in the sky.)

All of these graphic, vivid accounts of the "Miracle of FATIMA"

are by persons who were there at the actual time of the event on October 13, 1917. They witnessed it happen. We may as well try to abolish electricity and its use as to try to wipe out the story of this wondrous super-normal event by saying it didn't happen.

I call your attention now to a vital point. The movements of the so-called 'sun' at the Cova were "brusque" (quick, with sudden changes of direction). Those of you who have actually witnessed any unidentified flying objects (UFO's) in the sky at some time or other, have very likely noticed this type of movement in the objec It is unlike anything we can note in any earthbuilt vehicles desig ed for spaceflight today. It is a unique characteristic.

For instance, at Harmony Grove near Escondido, California, o July 4th, 1960, a UFO made an appearance in the sky near the camp ground where many students of this UFO subject were then assembled for their annual convention.* I was among the group at the time, and we observed the UFO as it maneuvered overhead. The object appeared to be disc-shaped, and as it moved, made brusque movements as well as long, smooth, gliding movements.

These movements of the UFO showed intelligent guidance. In my opinion, they are almost identical in resemblance to the movements of the so-called 'sun' at the Cova on Oct. 13, 1917. If you will recall, one eye witness of the Fatima Miracle described the sky object as a "crown of fire, empty in the middle". So now let us recall the sky object that we saw at Harmony Grove in 1960 -- the sighting is well documented by witnesses -- which also had a ring of brilliant light, bright as fire. It appeared to glow like a white neon light. This strong bright light was around a darker center, which gave somewhat the same effect of being empty in the middle.

In Russia, the question that was recently flung at the Soviet scientists was this: "Is the USSR convinced that there are or are not any UFO (Unidentified Flying Objects) in the skies?"

And the reply was this: "Soviet scientists maintain that no such objects exist. They believe that all UFO sightings are explained either by optical phenomena -- sun, clouds, temperature inversions -- or actual known objects such as planes, reflections from them, weather balloons, rockets and artificial Sputnicks."

That is the official Soviet Policy regarding UFO's. I believe you will admit at once that such a policy is loudly denying a vast portion of Reality as it exists in the "infiniverse". It is purest "egotism" to flatly state: No such objects exist. No man can so state until he goes out far beyond earth into interstellar space and looks over a few zillion other worlds. One does not need to do that if he will only be humble enough to look up often enough and at the right times. Having once seen a true spaceship not of this earth, one can never forget. Nor can one be doubtful again.

*Full details are
given in a previous   - 16 -
book: The Spacemasters
Speak. Published 1960.

FORCES THAT ARE OPPOSING MAN

Chapter Four

Earthman is being tested spiritually by certain forces which
seem to oppose him at every turn. Man's very soul progress is
being resisted -- day and night -- by opposing forces which are
within man himself. What are these force:
Basically, they are three in number.
The first is: Impure desires and craving:
for physical sensation. The second is:
Material illusion causing one to believe
that only matter is real. And the third
is: Egotism which ignores the fact of a
Supreme Creator in and behind Creation.

In this talk I am going to ask you
to humor me by imagining that each one of
the three forces is a personality. In
other words, we shall give a name to each
force and then as we go along we simply
use the name rather than a series of words
This makes our study easier. So the three
"code names" are as follows. (1) Lucifer = Impure desires, (2)
Ahriman = Material Illusion, (3) Asura = Personal Egotism.

These code names are valuable aids because they serve to iden-
tify in a brief, compact way the "lower elements" in every human
being. They represent the down-pulling desires and appetites, the
false thinking of the mind or intellect, and the "bloated" ego.

Life may be considered to be a "soul-testing" game we play
while we are here on planet Earth. In order to have a game, or
game conditions, we must have opponents...an adversary. In our
case, the adversary is the low-vibrating elements in us. The code
names being Lucifer, Ahriman and Asura. The game "started" when we
were born. Now if we give in to the adversary we get a "flunk",
which we realize in the form of unhappy, painful experiences.

But if we gain sufficient inner power to control the adversary -- thereby overcoming him -- we get a "win". The more "wins"
to our credit, even the small wins, the easier it is to get larger
more important wins, and the happier, more effective we are in life

How strong and masterful would we become without resistance
from these lower elements? Not very. You know we could simply go
on our merry way in life without bothering about these things at
all, without attending good lectures or reading good books. We
could just forget all about "overcoming" and not do anything con-
structive for our individual soul progress -- and then die..as mor-
tals do. We'd then go back to our Heavenly home where St. Peter is
waiting for us at the pearly gate. He lets us in with rejoicing.

- 17 -

We go to the Father, and the Father looks at us and asks: "Did you overcome the forces of Ahriman (material illusion) and break the rule of the deceiver, and lift up all the lower elements of the adversary within yourself and restore those elements to the Light of My Divine Plan?"

We answer lamely: "no, I didn't quite make it."

"Well then," replies the Father, "the Game is not over yet." And He lets us out through the back gate of Heaven, ships us down to the Earth again, and we start all over at the same old Game.

Now I am going to speak a little bit about a subject you've been hearing a great deal about recently, and that subject is Communism. It relates, you see, to this topic of the FATIMA MESSAGE, and shows why it is of such world importance. We wish to see what is really back of the idea of Communism and how the Communistic system of world conquest, subjugation and control, is but a tangible extension of an insidious and deadly "Ahrimanic" influence.

Back in 1909, long before Communism (as we know it today) ever got off the ground, the great spiritual teacher Dr. Rudolph Steiner had stated clearly in his early writings, a startling idea. He said that the forces of Ahriman and Asura would -- during our present modern age -- enter into the constitution of man to oppose the upward spiritual evolution of Earth's humanity, more intensely.

And what is the fact? Today the Ahriman and Asura forces are deceiving man in two ways. (1) They are persuading him that his innermost self -- his Real "I" -- is merely the resulting product of a material environment. Matter alone is real, and there is no such thing as a spirit or soul in man. (2) They are luring him into a belief in "Dialectic Materialism", the concept that unless you are able to perceive something by means of SENSE-DATA, it is not a valid part of Reality. On top of this concept, there is included a complete rejection of any belief in a Supreme Being.

Do we not see these identical aims embodied in the Communist Plan today? Under that system, men, women and children are being blinded to the reality of the Supreme Being and their own higher nature which is essentially spiritual and of God.

Quite frankly, we have all been more or less blinded by the "illusions" of Ahriman. This whole Piscean Age (of some 2000 years) which we have now come through, has had as its keynote: DECEPTION. Deception leads to Self-Undoing. Man has been very busy "undoing" himself through his self-deceiving practices as well as by the deceitful actions of other human beings whom he trusted. Why? Because man had to go through a "prep-training" course. He had to undergo a preliminary phase of learning before he could enter into the next higher phase. That phase of course is the AQUARIAN AGE, during which Man will receive his great "Initiation" into the light

of higher truth and his real liberation of spirit. This new phase
will be a time of spiritual understanding and freedom for man. A
time when the spirit of man will regain true dominion over matter..
and not the reverse. We shall have broken the rule of old, devil-
ish Ahriman.

"Reality," writes Stephen B. Miles, Jr., in an article which
appeared in the May, 1961 issue of "The Freeman", "started slipping
away from us when we allowed the early scientists to define it in
such a way as to exclude everything that couldn't be derived from
SENSE-DATA. This ushered in the reign of materialism, on which
Communism, the welfare state, progressive education, and most of
the other fallacies, chimeras, and delusions of our times are based
..." From the condition things are in today -- all over the world
-- it is clear to see that we need a better definition of what is
real...and what isn't.

Some people believe that "apparitions" are real...That super-
normal visions are a part of the reality we perceive only when a
few of our higher senses -- beyond the ordinary five -- are tuned
up and awakened. I happen to be one of those who believe this.

An apparition was recently perceived by both my wife Violet
and myself. I shall tell you about it because I believe it has a
bearing upon the subject we are vitally interested in...the Lady
of Fatima and her world secret. Do you remember the month of November, 1961, when a great fire started in the Santa Monica Mount-
ains of California? If you will recall, it burned and destroyed
not only 25,000 acres of valuable trees but also 400-500 homes in
Bel Air. This fire was a terrible shock to Southern California.

At the time this terrible fire occurred, I hadn't the slightest interest in the reported appearances of a mysterious "Lady" at
Fatima. I did not even know where the town of Fatima was located.
Nor did I know that this amazing Lady has made many such appearances in various parts of the world, at times of great CRISIS such
as these very times we are living in now.

On that startling Monday evening of November 6th, Violet and I
were watching the frightening development of the Bel-Air fire from
a safe distance at home -- for TV Channel 5 was televising pictures
of the awesome event. Imagine yourself now looking at "on-the-spot"
movie scenes of that fire, via your own TV screen and you have a
good idea of how Violet and I felt as we watched the uncontrolled
holocaust. (We could also see the flames from our home windows!)

Suddenly, a clear image of a Lady -- the entire full figure --
appeared on the television screen before our eyes. "She" was standing, apparently, in the very midst of those ravaging flames, her
arms outstretched as if sending a protective blessing over the area.
She was dressed in a full robe which had a mantle that covered her
head and shoulders, so that her face was not distinctly seen by us.

In astonishment I viewed this amazing apparition, realizing that
here indeed was a super-normal phenomenon. It was certainly not
being "staged" for the public by the Television Station. Turning
quickly to Violet, I asked one question: "Do you see anything unusual on the TV screen?" She answered, "Yes! I do see something!
It's the robed figure of a lady -- of Mary!"

We watched the "Lady" for three minutes. When first we saw
her, she was standing sideways, arms outstretched in blessing.
Then minutes later she turned very slowly, facing toward us, and
quietly faded out of view. The "apparition" was over. It had mad
a profound impression upon me and upon Violet, I can assure you.
We determined to find out all we could about the "Lady", her various appearances in the world and what her great mission is.

This astonishing event -- our apparition -- triggered a most
dedicated search. The search led us straight to the documented
case of the apparitions at Fatima, the miracle of the so-called
'sun' before the awe-struck gaze of 70,000 people at the Cova da
Iria. It caused us to read and study the FATIMA MESSAGE given by
the marvelous Lady to Lucy, Jacinta and Francisco in July of 1917.

In Portugal, at the little town of Leiria, lives a Bishop.
When Lucy Santos first received the highly secret "third part" of
the now-famous Fatima Message, she entrusted it to the Bishop of
Leiria for safekeeping. It was then arranged that this final portion -- the secret -- was to be opened and read in May of 1960. Or,
if for any reason Lucy should happen to die before that date, the
message was to be opened and read at the time of her death.

May, 1960 came...and went. What happened? Nothing. For some
mysterious reason the "third part" of the Fatima Message remains a
deep, dark mystery to the world's humanity. Logically, we may now
assume that at least a few persons know what that secret is. One
individual who undoubtedly knows the "secret" -- having doubtless
read it in May, 1960 -- is the good Bishop of Leiria.

A few months ago the Bishop of Leiria came to visit Los Angele:
California. (Who doesn't at one time or another?) Although this
Bishop is not the same one who originally placed the controversial
Fatima Message in his church archives for safekeeping, he is the
present Bishop of Leiria. His power and authority are the same as
that of the previous Bishop, who, by the way, has in the interim
between 1917 and 1960, passed on to his heavenly reward. The present Bishop of Leiria now has official charge of the "secret".

On arriving in Los Angeles, the Bishop paid a brief visit to
church friends of his in the nearby town of Artesia. There is a
small settlement of Portuguese-speaking people in that town, and so
he spent some time mingling with those individuals at the local
church. When asked to tell some details of the "Fatima Secret",
the Bishop replied that the secret has been blown up in some persons' imaginations to an extent that is all out of proportion to

what it really is. He cautioned his listeners not to believe all
the wild stories that are going around.

My friend, do you wonder -- as I do -- why he did not put an
end to those wild stories right then and there...by simply revealing to his listeners the real nature of the Fatima Secret? Would
it not have been perfectly easy for him to have cleared up the
whole controversy -- the world-wide misunderstanding about it --
by the very natural act of reading the now-opened message???

Of course you do. But he may be "under orders" not to reveal
the contents of the third part of the Fatima Message, for reasons
we need not concern ourselves with now. Our attention at this pre-
cise moment, is more involved with the Secret itself. Now, this
Secret did not prophesy that the threat of world domination by
Communism coming out of Russia would completely take over all of
the free world, because the Lady has said in the second part of
her Message that "In the end my Immaculate Heart will triumph, and
Russia will be converted." Therefore, we can write-off the boast
of Nikita Kruschchev that: "The total world will be Communistic by
1981.." as one prediction that will never happen on Earth.

What then, could this Fatima Secret consist of? Utopia? End
of the world? Cataclysms in Canada? Sudden death of the Pope by
martyrdom? Collapse of the Catholic Church? The coming forth of
"Abominable Men" such as the "Big Foot" and the "Sasquatch" out of
their caves under the earth to take over control of the world? In-
vasion of the world by people from outer space? Etc., etc. etc.

I am positive that we need not expect to find that the Secret
predicts a serenely peaceful, happy-go-lucky, easy cream-puff kind
of future for mankind. That comes later when and if we earn it.

Neither should we start developing a bad case of "Dooms-Day
Jitters" and be feverishly reaching for our "tranquillizers" --
"happy pills" -- and the nearest "head shrinker" because we know
this is it. The world is about to end (again)...! You may take
it from me, or better yet, from Lucy Santos herself...that is definitely NOT WHAT THE GLORIOUS, SPARKLING LADY REVEALED to her.

Quite true, Lucy did predict with perfect accuracy the great
"miracle" that occurred on October 13, 1917...an event witnessed
by more than 70,000 persons. But we should remember that humans
as a species are not infallible. They can -- and often do -- make
mistakes. Lucy is only human. Therefore Lucy is not infallible.
She could be wrong about the idea -- whatever that idea may be --
expressed in the mysterious third part of the Fatima Message.

However, since it is true that she was 100% right in her forecast regarding the October 13th event as revealed in the publicly
known part of the Message, it is more than probable that whatever
is forecast by the secret third part of the Message is also right.

21

WHAT IS THE FATIMA SECRET?

Chapter Five

I think it would be well to mention -- before going further in our dedicated search for light on the great Fatima Secret -- that we have no "axes" to grind. By this I mean that I am not interested in setting out to prove that you are "in the wrong", or that the church is wrong, or that I am wrong about anything.

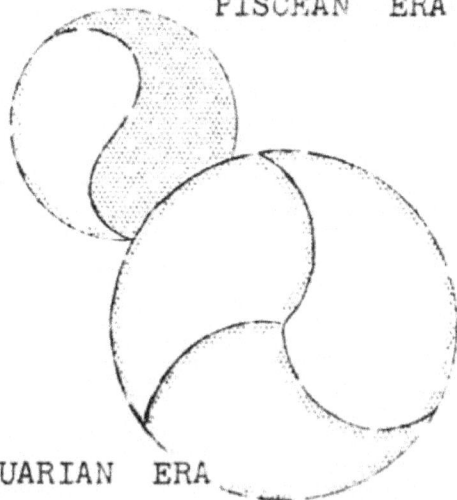

PISCEAN ERA

AQUARIAN ERA

We are simply interested in getting to the bottom of a mystery. We want to discover what the Fatima Secret is. The important thing we seek is the Truth -- Knowingness -- if such can be had.

However, on this subject of what is contained in the third part of the Fatima Message, we face what seems to be quite a problem. Namely, it is this: Suppose you had viewed with your own eyes a clear apparition of a feminine figure suddenly appearing on the screen of your TV set, while you are watching the televising of a terrible fire that is consuming hundreds of homes. And if you perceived that this being was "Our Lady" -- how would you feel?

Admittedly, it was a "private revelation". Or more accurately "semi-private", since the identical apparition was also seen then by my wife, Violet. The theory that it might have been a hallucination can be ruled out on the grounds that two individuals saw the same image during the same time interval. That image, coming when it did and in such a unique manner, exerted an unusually impelling pressure upon us both...for to Violet and me, a "sign" had been given. We would follow where that sign would lead us.

It led us -- swiftly and irrevocably -- into this fabulous adventure, this relentless search for an answer to the great enigma of THE WORLD SECRET OF FATIMA. But how -- in the name of heaven and all that is holy -- do you go about finding that answer?

Do you read all the "Fatima Books"? Listen to every wild rumor purporting to reveal the mystery of the "Third Part" of Our Lady's Message? Yes, all that might help. But would it really give you an answer that is fully satisfying to your inner self?

Do you hop a jet plane, roar off in the direction of Portugal, land at Fatima (near the center of Portugal) hop out and then look up the Bishop of Leiria with the object of getting him to open up the archive and show you the secret part of the FATIMA MESSAGE? You could, if you could afford the trip and could talk Portuguese.

But would that method of action really prove as resultful as you had hoped? The fact is, numerous authors, researchers and publishers have tried that particular way already. Result? All they came home with after their long trip to far-off Portugal was merely more exasperating theories, educated guesses, and a few photographs of the beautiful Shrine of Fatima.

You see, all of us researchers for the WORLD SECRET OF FATIMA are in agreement on one major point. We shall play the game according to certain gentlemanly rules of fair play. Very well. That means that physically stealing the secret message away from the custodian of it -- the Bishop of Leiria -- is against the rules... Any use of physical force is "outside" of the rules. It would not be right nor fair, for example, for you or for me to criminally assault the good Bishop, tie him up so he is helpless, and force him at the point of a snubnosed automatic to "hand over the famous secret of Fatima to us...or else!"

What alternative action, then, is left open to us? Is the secret beyond our discovery? Is it truly an insuperable problem, impossible of solution by the human mind? Should we admit that the mystery is inscrutable, and give up the search for an answer?

We could. But wait! A most intriguing idea is forming within our mind this very minute. A "key" to the mystery is being given to us, mentally. We recall elatedly that it was by influence of a "private revelation" that we originally started out on this strange quest for the FATIMA SECRET. Could it be that by the simple expediency of invoking another "private revelation" -- dealing specifically with the hidden contents of the FATIMA MESSAGE, the same document which at this moment seems so secure within the church archives of the Bishop of Leiria -- we might fathom that fascinating Secret? Impossible? Who can say what is impossible.

Not that I should expect officials of churchdom, nor for that matter, anyone other than my closest friends, to accept such a revelation. No. However, if such an inner revelation were given me in such a manner as to deeply impress my very soul, arousing within me a true sense of reality...and if it truly enlightened me..then I would thank God for it and for its soul-satisfying Light.

It was November 7, the night that the terrifying fire was finally controlled. I had spent most of the day in research, and at night, just before going to sleep, while my body was relaxing comfortably, I decided to send up a mental request to my higher self. I requested a positive answer to the mystery of the Fatima Secret.

I realized, as no doubt you also realize, that physical limitations mean nothing to the higher self, the real spirit of man... It is entirely possible for man's spirit to free itself occasionally from the confines of the physical body, travel to any desired region of this planet, and obtain "direct-knowingness" of any given

object. There is a "Knower" indwelling in each of us. We can, in times of real need, contact it for purposes of higher instruction provided our "communication lines" to it are open and clear.

In the early hours of the very next morning, just prior to sunrise, I awakened with the following message running through my mind:

"THE WORLD, BY THE APPEARANCE OF MARY, WILL BE AWAKENED
TO THE COMING OF THE CHRIST..."

Each word of the message impressed itself powerfully upon my mental awareness, almost as if some unseen higher being were close by and speaking to me with concentrated intent and purpose.

It was a simple message...beautifully direct. It is for you, just as much as it is for me and for the whole world. See if you do not find some very special meaning just for you in those lighted words. I am certain you shall. For you will note that the message contains both the Madonna idea and the Messiah idea; and it relates these to "the world" of mankind. Who can say that these ideas are not deep and wide...solemn and mystic?

Man cannot save himself. Mary must help; a Madonna must come to the rescue. In other words, Divinity, God in Man, is not masculine alone. There is also a Divine Feminine principle in man and great is its power to preserve, to love, to heal and to balance. Mary is the universal symbol of the Divine Feminine idea -- in essence, the perfected human soul. Mary as principle says: "I LOVE LIFE!"

A person, all unaware that he is a Soul, scarcely more than exists. He passes listlessly through earthlife and is not inspired by a high and exalting mental impulse. I have ancient books calling this state, "Widowhood of the Soul". This term is highly accurate as a figure of speech. "Widowhood of the Soul" implies a loss. The symbol is of a widow in deep mourning, in sombre black, and her robes are not those of the "woman clothed with the sun".

The "sun" in symbology signifies "spirit". When the human Soul -- woman dressed in sombre, black robes -- is gently guided out into the "Sun" (Spirit) she becomes "clothed with the sun".

She then gives birth to the "Christ" or perfected human spirit in man. This is the real Christ-idea as it applies to all men, all women; for it is the glorious destiny which all may share.

Say what one will...ignore, cast aside, avoid, forget, or do what one may...the real, Christ-idea (Divine Life, Love, Light in each human being, equilibrated)...not the current mechanical notion that Divinity is beyond our reach...is the deepest, truest and highest idea ever set within the human soul. All things human really revolve around the soul. We cannot live, we cannot love and we cannot think without using powers of the Soul within us. Earthman,

however, has insulted the pure Reality of his own Soul (Life, Love, Light) by ignoring it in an insane clutching for money and material power. All that the masculine powers can _see_ is money and material power. The feminine powers behold the Soul. And Soul...is coming into its own!

"THE WORLD, BY THE APPEARANCE OF MARY, WILL BE AWAKENED
TO THE COMING OF THE CHRIST..."

I interpret this to signify that a new Reign of Soul is about to commence on this planet. This is not something similar to current religions. Awareness of Soul and its qualities will steadily lift individuals to progressively higher levels of spiritual truth. This increase of Soul-Awareness will awaken man to Christ-Consciousness, for the Prince of Man, in the fulness of time, will appear in his kingdom.

Mary, blessed Madonna of the Christ-Light, is working now to prepare us all for what is coming. Doubtless she shall make many more appearances by means of spiritual "apparitions" permitting various individuals to recognize and assist her spiritually. She will also demonstrate her power by working directly through Nature. This...is terribly important. The Divine Mother desires to restore harmony within all physical creation. How may she do this? By bringing about certain controlled reactions within Nature first, which will assist in restoring balance among Nature's elements and at the same time cause man to "wake up" to one simple fact. Something is terribly wrong -- hence -- the Divine hand is intervening.

Human souls -- yours, mine, and the souls of 3+ billion other inhabitants on this earth -- are constantly thinking, feeling and acting. By so doing, we are creating vibrations in the very ethers of this planet. We are sending those vibrations into the very soul of the Earth itself. _We are affecting its soul_. For we are capable of either raising or lowering the vibrations of the subtle, etheric envelope (aura) which surrounds the earth. An example?

If you habitually think of yourself as "weak, pale and sick", your thoughts are impressing as negative vibrations upon your soul, which in turn reacts by reflecting those actual conditions in your physical body. Result: You really _become_ weak, pale, sick.

In the very same way, the bad thoughts of men -- greed, mass hatred, envy, etc. -- plus outright destructive actions such as the violence killings and the "A" & "H"-bomb explosions, have hurt the very soul of our planet. By the end of 1961, Soviet Russia had exploded more than 25 A-Bombs in the atmosphere, including a superbomb in excess of 50-megatons. Most of the U.S. testing has been underground. But official decision now is to resume nuclear bomb tests in air. This may be a necessary decision, but it is a deplorable one. Even the hard-headed scientists admit we "may never know the full effects of the Hydrogen bomb tests." We do, however, know one thing now.

We know this: A reaction from Nature is beginning to manifest all over the world in order that harmony may be established within the natural realm; this is awakening humanity soulwise and spiritwise.

Something big is ahead for earthman, and he cannot cognize it unless he "wakes up" his Soul first. To help speed up this waking up process, the soul of Nature must take a much more active role in the affairs of humanity. Therefore, many unusual conditions of Nature in the form of extraordinary disturbances of the Earth may now be expected to occur. It is, in fact, already underway.

Please note carefully what I am saying here. I do not wish to have you misinterpret what I am telling you. A world period of extraordinary disturbances on the part of Mother Nature is now in effect. By this I do not mean "total catastrophe", "immediate doom", nor the "end of the world". Nothing like that is being stated. It is definitely and most decidedly not the "end of the world"!

All right. Beginning with the latter part of 1961, a definite and noticeable acceleration or "stepping-up" of reaction on the part of Nature has occurred. Sudden, radical and drastic changes in climate have been felt by man. Bad weather -- abnormally severe -- rainstorms that hit like deluges. Floods, hurricanes, tornadoes, roaring forest fires, earthquakes, blizzards and below-zero freezing spells in various parts of the globe. World-wide. This is it. It is the real beginning of the reaction period of Mother Nature. Look at it this way. Action = reaction. Reaction = action. Man has acted destructively and now Nature is reacting and in the process she is removing those persons who are karmically unfit for life in the non-destructive New Age. We must realize it. Must realize:

"THE WORLD, BY THE APPEARANCE of MARY, WILL BE AWAKENED
TO THE COMING OF THE CHRIST..."

My friend, here is real food for thought. The many human lives that were suddenly swept away recently through wars, bloody riots, earthquakes, tidal waves, floods, fierce storms, hurricanes and by other causes, were those who did not belong to this dispensation we are now entering. They must be prepared for rebirth in the dispensation to come later. When Jesus of Nazareth was among us, he said to the ones who could not understand, "Ye are not my sheep; therefore, ye believe me not." All such will ripen in another dispensation and be the fruits of the next Messiah.

The world at the present time is passing through a regenerating and purifying process. All the darkness and selfishness must become transformed into understanding and right activity. Already the minds and hearts of humanity are stirred; the chosen number are now awakened, AWARE that something is happening, but do not yet know just what it is. It will not be long until the Real Light will appear in all its glory. Then the whole world will turn their minds toward higher ideals, seeking the Light consciously and voluntarily.

When Jesus walked the hills of Galilee with his disciples, the Sign of the Fishes -- the Piscean Age -- had begun to flourish. Duality was ruling in men's consciousness. "Yang and "Yin" or Positive vs. Negative, was the order of the day. The law was "an eye for an eye and a tooth for a tooth". Result was <u>conflict</u> <u>and</u> <u>deception</u>.

OLD
PISCES

=

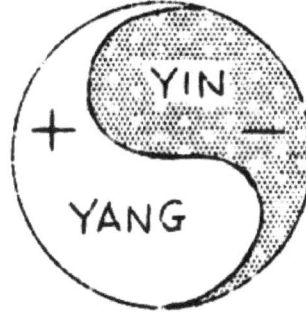

DUALITY
DECEPTION
<u>INHARMONY</u>

THE WORLD SECRET as we view it, is this: HUMANITY WILL OVERCOME THE OPPOSITES IN THE NEW ERA OF AQUARIUS BY "EQUILIBRATING" THEM. The word "equilibrate"means to bring about perfect equilibrium, balance, or harmony within two or more opposite conditions or forces. It is only by equilibrating, balancing the opposites that a <u>brand</u> <u>new</u> <u>condition,</u> <u>a</u> <u>"third"</u> <u>condition is created</u>. Duality then vanishes and the essential Truth and Agreement appear.

NEW
AQUARIUS

=

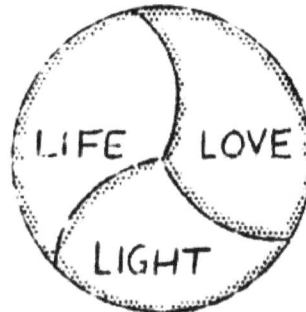

TRIUNE-ONENESS
<u>TRUTH</u>
HARMONY

Triune-Oneness = a balanced view of reality = Truth. This is the Secret in which all men may share in the New Era. It is not limited to one man, but open to all. It can transform the world by putting man back on the right course. This basic idea is so simple yet so potent, it seems "dangerous" to some. Those individuals, institutions and governments who now function by <u>deceiving</u>, shall become increasingly powerless as man grasps and applies this principle. For Truth alone is power, and when it appears the false cannot survive. No wonder some would like this secret kept forever hidden!

But mark this. A NEW ERA OF BROTHERHOOD IN HUMAN SOCIETY UPON EARTH IS ABOUT TO DAWN... ALREADY MILLIONS OF US ARE WELCOMING THE COMING OF THE PRINCIPLE OF TRUTH. WE ARE ON THE MARCH, AND NOTHING CAN STOP US NOW. WE ARE BLENDING DUALITY INTO A NEW CONDITION! THE NEW SYMBOL OF <u>TRIUNE ONENESS</u> IS NOW TO BECOME <u>ACTIVE</u> IN THE CONSCIOUS NESS OF MEN!

WE DELVE DEEPER AND DEEPER

Chapter Six

The one thing all the world is seeking is Truth. This is the "Pearl of Great Price" which we are told by the wise to "search for as for hid treasures". Why? Because only by finding Truth can we satisfy the hunger of the Soul.

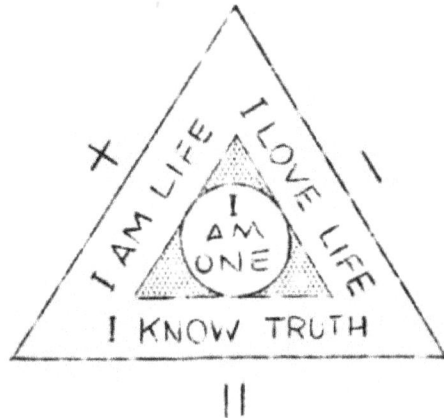

What is the Soul hungry for? If we still ourselves for a moment the answer comes: The Soul wants more freedom from the world illusion that "Matter is boss". The Soul that is you yearns to be recognized as a Spiritual Being with all the rights, powers, authority and responsibility of a true Spiritual Being.

Your Soul wants to "triumph over Matter" and see itself reflected in the real mirror of life as the image and likeness of God. This is the great object or goal of your life upon material planets. Day by day, life by life, the light of your Soul increases little by little. By this I mean that as you continue your earth experiences in a material, flesh body, there is a very gradual rise in your level of "beingness". It is as if you were awakening spiritually..seeing your Real Self for the first time and getting a clearer idea of who and what you really are.

You go to sleep every night. But, when you are asleep, are you aware that you are sleeping? No.(Unless you are a person who has developed this unusual faculty of knowing.) You only know at the moment of awakening, that you were asleep. The same thing is true of human souls in physical bodies. Those souls are not aware of "beingness" until they have "awakened" from sleep...in matter.

Matter is just like a veil over the soul. It keeps you from seeing the Real You. When veiled in matter, the soul is conscious only of existence. When the veil is lifted -- even partially -- the innermost light, "Spirit" is again revealed in its glory. The Soul then awakens and becomes aware of its divine beingness. Our Lady, by her various appearances in apparitions and through Nature's stern reactions, is now causing vast numbers of humanity to become less conscious of "mere existence", and more and more conscious of being. This is the essential mission of the Madonna.

"THE WORLD, BY THE APPEARANCE OF MARY," (The Divine Mother principle of: "I Love Life") "WILL BE AWAKENED TO THE COMING OF THE CHRIST." Here is the gist of the real Fatima Secret. Before man can have the most intimate contact with Reality (Truth on the level of eternal principles) so that he may become truly wise, he must first embrace the higher principle: "I Love Life in all its forms!"

How, then, can we embrace this higher principle ("I Love Life in all its forms") in a practical way? We look at ourselves in the mirror each morning and realize that WE ARE ALIVE. Good. Each of us says, "I Am alive". What we have forgotten to do is to ask the basic, vitally important question we should dare to ask: "How alive am I?" We assumed that the Divine Viewpoint -- our real "I" within us -- had been allotted a certain limited quota of Life-force and that no more could be made available. This was our big error.

We, as a human race, have said: Life equals Power. And we know that we wanted more of it. We wanted it for survival and for evolving. For we knew deep down inside that we must perfect ourselves as beings. But--not knowing what "Power" really meant, we substituted "Force" as our goal and spent thousands of years using force upon one another. That didn't, however, increase our individual allotments of Life. It actually depressed our Life, decreased our "Beingness". As an example today, the Atom Bomb = FORCE = Depression of Life in all living forms which receive its blast or fallout

Power really means a "balanced expression of force", rather than an unbalanced expression. Power heals. It doesn't depress Life; balanced Power LOVES LIFE. Power uses force in a manner that helps, not hinders, the "Beingness" in all life forms. It does not use force in a way that depletes or takes the life from man. The truth is, "Life" in you can be INCREASED to such a tremendous degree over what it now is, that the difference between the present-appearing you and the you with the Life-plus, would be markedly noticeable in the way you look, think, feel, act and appear to others. Interesting?

How does this fit in with the promise of the Master: "I came that ye might have LIFE and have IT more ABUNDANTLY." Food for thought, is it not? How then, may we have more LIFE? By developing an affinity, or a close attraction or real love for...Life. We must become a magnet for Life--for BEINGNESS. We must say, "I LOVE LIFE! For this is the Divine Mother principle (loving life). This is the spiritual attribute which Mary personifies. As a Divine principle, Mary is co-equal with the Father principle itself. In the non-dual state of being which is the true Power, we find the abundant life. The action of LOVE moves us toward this non-duality state, wherein is the real Power, or LIFE ABUNDANT.

The spiritual attribute which Mary personifies IS this LOVE of Life--this is the divine feminine or Divine Mother principle.

The Father Principle is: I AM LIFE (Divine Masculine)
The Mother Principle is: I LOVE LIFE (Divine Feminine)
Both principles are absolutely co-equal, as illustrated here.

FATHER		MOTHER
+		-
"I AM LIFE,		"I LOVE LIFE,
I AM BEINGNESS"	=	I LOVE BEINGNESS"

The "Secret" is that "Mary" (as principle) must appear within Earthman's human consciousness before the "Christ-spirit" can manifest itself. Why? Because the Mother principle: "I Love Life" is co-equal with the Father principle in the Divine Trinity of the Father-Mother-Son. Man has not appreciated nor seen the immense value of the Mother principle -- an intense affinity for Life and Beingness -- and so has refused to grant to other bodies the important right to "Be".

"Affinity" means a close attraction or "related by marriage" state. The two principles: Mother-Father, Negative-Positive, are intended to work closely together as Power. But you see how unbalanced is man's use of Life. Man is saying, "I am Life!"; but he is neglecting to say, "I Love Life Be-ingness and I extend my love to include all Beings. I grant to all life forms the right to BE!"

The churches have stressed the Father principle which is the masculine principle (I am Life). A few of them such as the Catholic Church and the Christian Science Church do emphasize the Mother Principle, but do not interpret it in the simple, "I Love Life" formula. The Protestants left it out entirely. However, until more of orthodox churchianity is willing to include it in their doctrine, their teaching will continue to be unbalanced and feeble.

The principle of "fire" was around since the beginning of all creation, but man did not wake up to the fact that it existed until one day he saw it in action, caught a bit of it and put it to use. That is how it is with the Divine Mother principle. It is there -- waiting for us to discover it so that our lives may be transformed.

Now the Truth is this: When "awakened" human beings permit the Mother-Father principles of "I am Life + I Love Life" to cooperate within their Human consciousness, a new and perfectly balanced POWER-PRINCIPLE is born of that union. It is called the "Son" or the "Christ-Spirit" or simply the "Essential Christ".

All religions are good...to the extent that they succeed in connecting man up with his true source of Life, Love and Light... in Balance, so that he can actually demonstrate the God-Power. But if they are not doing that, of what spiritual benefit are they?

The time has come when Religion must be scientific, and Science must be religious. Both must "bear witness to the Truth" for the simple reason that Earthman is growing up. Man is exploring space (both inner and outer) and thinking individuals want to be told the Truth, the whole Truth, and nothing but the Truth...or else..they will stop going to churches and will find Truth elsewhere.

With the now-dawning New Age comes the recognition by man of the sacred rule that every Soul is perfectly free to Be, Do and Have this "Essential Christ-Spirit" of Life, Love and Light in a more abundant measure than we have ever dreamed possible to Man.

Chapter Seven

I think we are ready now to "add-up" in your own mind all of the things we have been giving consideration to in this important study of the Fatima Message, and see what it really means to you. This will prove very helpful. It will not only assist in clarifying the world significance of the "Secret" itself, but also it can enable you to derive practical help for Body, Mind and Soul.

As we look back momentarily -- the wonderful story of Lucy, Jacinta and Francisco and the whole Fatima episode of seeming miracles -- is ours once more to enjoy. We are "re-living" it all again: The marvelous apparitions of the glorious Celestial Youth and the appearances of Mary to the children...The mean action of the magistrate of Fatima in jailing the three little ones....The doubting parents who did not believe...The priest looking anxiously at his watch...And the actual witnessing of a strange, glowing object in the sky by 70,000 awestruck human beings. Wonderful!

What does it all signify? It signifies that earthman is not alone, nor is he the highest product of God's Creation. There also exist other beings who are alive and functioning in this great universe, but obviously upon a higher vibrational level than ours.

Why the apparitions? To awaken man. There is an entirely REAL and very beautiful Soul-World all around us, with people living in that Soul-World. Yet we are not "awake" nor "aware" of its reality and beingness. The vast Soul-World is as clearly visible to one who has discovered his own Soul, and how to use it, as the physical world is to our eyes. You may rest absolutely sure and certain that you are a Soul. Also, that after you leave your human body (which is not _you_) you will inhabit that populous realm.

Fantastic? Far-fetched? Impossible? Science says there is a vibrational belt or "Spectrum" in the universe, and that spectrum consists of ever ascending rates of vibration. They tell us that the Ultimate Reality we call God has constructed this "Infinite Spectrum" out of His own Beingness. Drs. Albert Einstein and Chas. Steinmetz have concluded this is a true hypothesis and have often referred to this great spectrum of color-ray vibrations from "0" to Infinity, of which the _human_ consciousness can perceive but a tiny portion. However, Man can, while yet in a flesh body, raise his consciousness -- his perception -- and so go "up-scale".

At a high enough point on the scale, you or I could actually look into the Soul-World. Even enter it and travel around there. In that realm you would gain _reality_ on many now-mysterious subjects. "Flying Saucers", for example, would be made clear to you. The very first step toward the perception of more of this Truth comes with Soul-Unfoldment. And one of the first steps you can take _now_ is to _increase Beingness_.

I would like -- with your agreement -- to have you practice a very simple but potent soul-drill. The object of it is to scientifically increase your individual beingness. In the list below, a series of different beings are indicated. What I wish you to do is (1) Read the listed words, taking them slowly, one at a time. For example: "MY FATHER". Check your inward feeling as you say it. (2) State aloud how much beingness (freedom to be, live and express life) you are now willing to grant that being... much, some, little, or none

(3) State aloud the distance from you that you are willing to permit that being to come, before his nearness makes you uncomfortable. For example: Do you feel all right about his being on the same planet with you? The same nation, same state, city, house? And for how long? Illustration: "MY FATHER" I am willing to grant him a great deal of beingness. I am comfortable whenever he is in this Nation, or in this State, or in this City. I am willing to allow him to enter my home and remain with me ? months, (days or hours

If You are now ready, please start the Beingness Drill.

Part One. Personal

1. MYSELF
2. MY FATHER
3. MY MOTHER
4. MY BROTHERS
5. MY SISTERS
6. MY HUSBAND
7. MY WIFE
8. MY CHILDREN
9. MY FATHER-IN-LAW
10. MY MOTHER-IN-LAW
11. MY AUNTS
12. MY UNCLES
13. MY COUSINS
14. MY FRIENDS
15. MY ENEMIES

Part Two. Impersonal

16. ALL ADULT HUMANS	24. ALL ANIMALS
17. SOME ADULT HUMANS	25. SOME ANIMALS
18. ALL CHILDREN	26. ALL BIRDS
19. SOME CHILDREN	27. SOME BIRDS
20. ALL HUMAN RACES	28. ALL REPTILES
21. SOME HUMAN RACES	29. SOME REPTILES
22. ALL INSECTS	30. ALL FISH
23. SOME INSECTS	31. SOME FISH

SPECIAL NOTE: Perform this drill three times a week for two weeks. Make an effort to grant more beingness each time. The results of granting beingness to others may surprise you pleasantly.

The Beingness Drill may be performed with another person's help. You can, for instance, have a close friend read the words on the list to you, while you do the granting of beingness. Make a game of it and you will find it fun, with or without assistance.

This is not merely a mental drill. It is a soul-drill, designed to aid, support and awaken you on the Soul level. Why? Very plainly, the fact is this. Time is now short before the New Dispensation must "lock into gear". This period is "wake-up time" for the world...spiritually. The next higher class in the Great School of Planetary Life is about to begin, and all New Age individuals who are really trying and who have "done their homework" (applied what they are given) will make the grade in joyous ease.

For those who remain loyal to the highest that is in them, there is no need for fear of the outer turmoil in the world. Fear not. Keep faith with me. We are all under higher protection. The children of earth are being prepared to enter a new and more spiritual period in the history of this planet, as we have now completed one-half of all the cycles through which earth will pass. We have traversed the appointed path and are now in the beginnings that reveal higher degrees of consciousness -- the divine light within...the Light of the Soul. A Soul Era is commencing on Earth.

And what is the "essence" of the Fatima Secret? In three words we could say: "BEINGNESS IN BALANCE". The Beingness Drill causes you to give more attention to the Mother Principle of Affinity; it brings it up into greater equality with the Father Principle. The result will be an inflow of more abundant Life into your body, mind and soul. Improvement will be noticed at once. It will continue to increase at every practice session. As your Beingness rises, your burdens will grow lighter, and lighter, and lighter.

When we realize that the real "I" in us is a spark of that Divine Trinity of Life, Love Light (Father-Mother-Son), and we start putting equal emphasis upon all THREE parts of that trio, instead of a heavy emphasis upon one or two parts and ignoring the other part, we discover to our great delight that we go "up-scale" very rapidly. Our perception rapidly increases and as it does, so does certainty. We are becoming able to know more truth on high levels.

The whole Cosmic Universe then become our "church"; all living creatures are its members. Our God is the Good in all creation and we consciously "know" our Good by realizing more "Beingness in Balance" every day. It is the "Life more Abundant" open to us all.

In the Old Era, love of the Soul was forgotten through love of the senses. But materiality has not solved our problems, only increased them. With help and direction from the Beautiful Madonna now hovering o'er earth's children, you and I can assist her in the unfolding of a Divine-Awareness on the earth. Let us vow that, in this New Age, the Image of the Divine Mother will again be restored!

* * * * * * THE - 33 - END * * * * * *

HANDY ORDER FORM

OTHER CONFIDENTIAL BOOKS BY MICHAEL X

☐ "FLYING SAUCER REVELATIONS" -- This is the FOUNDATION course for all students who seek greater knowledge of our Space Friends, on all levels. Five unusual and revealing sections contain valuable SECRETS for you. Postpaid $2.00

☐ "VENUSIAN HEALTH MAGIC" -- Here is a wondrous way of Life and Health..the way of the Wise Ones! A wealth of new, powerful and priceless information that may mean the transformation of your life. TEN big sections. Postpaid $5.00

☐ "VENUSIAN SECRET-SCIENCE" -- This Master Course contains secret truths regarding the planet VENUS, the marvelous Venusians and their advanced Science of LIFE, LOVE & LIGHT. 7 Wonderful, thrilling lessons. Postpaid $5.00

☐ "YOUR D-DAY DESTINY" -- Will the prophesied disaster, the "shaking terribly" of the earth and its polar flip really happen? This most unusual book gives you a truly enlightening PREVUE of your "Diploma Day" just ahead. $2.00

☐ "D-DAY SEERS SPEAK" -- Startling NEW information in this book gives you a clear picture - much clearer than ever before -- of things to come soon. It is packed with timely facts, instruction, guidance. Postpaid only $2.00

☐ "SECRETS OF HIGHER CONTACT" -- At last, here are the answers to your most vital, "Contact" questions! How do you get in touch with the Space People? What is the wisest procedure? SEVEN thrilling chapters. Postpaid only $2.00

☐ "RAINBOW CITY AND THE INNER EARTH PEOPLE" -- A fabulous city -- Rainbow City -- is said to be located beyond the South Pole, in Antarctica -- Is Rainbow City a secret Space Base for Inner Earth People? Vital data. Postpaid $2.00

* * * * * * * * * * * * *

HOW TO ORDER

Indicate with an X in squares at left, which of the books you want. Tear page out and mail it with your remittance to:

THE FUTURA PRESS
P. O. Box 34602   I am enclosing $...............
Los Angeles 34, Calif.

Name...

Address..

City...........................Zone...........State.............
If a resident of California add sales tax.